# The ]
# Dance ot Lite

## PRINCESS MAZZALOULOU

# THE BEAUTIFUL DANCE OF LIFE

PRINCESS MAZZALOULOU

# PRINCESS MAZZALOULOU

ISBN:

ISBN-13: 978-1533592521
ISBN-10: 1533592527

# DEDICATION

Jamie and Sonny

# ACKNOWLEDGMENTS

Thanks to Sonny, Jamie, and Buster

PRINCESS MAZZALOULOU

*Also by Princess Mazzaloulou*

*Free Your Inner Princess*
*The Power of Love Hearts*
*I Believe in a Life Lived with a Fairy Princess Heart*
*The Spirit of Princesses*

# INTRODUCTION

Balance in life is key to living well. We are physical beings, but
we came from the spiritual realm and continue to be spiritual
beings. However, the mind and the senses can lead us to
believe more in physical reality, and sometimes that can leave
us feeling powerless, fearful, and unworthy. The Universe can
guide us through life and weave a path that is personal and
magical for each of us, if we tune in and follow the signs. But,
as we begin the journey, it is important for us to be laying
down a solid foundation, so we can continue to build upon
layer after layer. Therefore, walking the path requires resources
of all kinds: faith, commitment, patience, strength, trust, and
faith. My aim, through the writing of this book, is to reinforce
the courage and belief in all princesses who are willing to take
on the very brave challenge of liberating themselves to make
small, or big, positive changes. We can learn to move through
the open window of life and free ourselves by connecting both
to the physical and the spiritual, for it is through the intuitive
balance of the two that we can leave behind fear and comfort
zones and live wholly and wonderfully. We deserve to live the
best lives, just like fairy tale princesses.

# THE BEAUTIFUL DANCE OF LIFE

PRINCESS MAZZALOULOU

*Princess in the morning*

In the early morning, the world feels silent and still, but there is a flow, an energy that is always evolving and flowing. It is within this flow of energy that life flourishes.

*On waking and stretching out my muscles, I activate the flow of the energy of the Universe within my body. I feel alive and connected to all that is wonderful. I am connected to the secrets and the miracles of the Universe that lie in each and every moment.*

*Princess reaching for the sky*

Trees are usually depicted as wise, strong, grounded, and solid. Being connected to the Earth via deep, powerful roots, we trust in the stability of mighty trees. We can imagine our being like strong, tall trees, reaching always for the sky, the sun, the light, and the warmth.

*I can stretch my body gently up to the sky, and feel light and free. Yet, I can imagine that from my solar plexus, I am connected deep within the Earth via strong, energetic roots. I can experience the best of both worlds and feel inner harmony as I go about my day and life.*

*Princess harnessing the secrets of the Universe*

If we are in tune and aligned with the energy of the Universe, then wonderful things can happen in our lives. Knowing the rules of the Universe can assist us in living life to the full. Letting go of control shows us that we often do not need to do anything in order to elicit change, for the Universe is always trying to take us down the correct path.

*I know the secrets and forces of the Universe: there is an energy that is so much more than me in my physical form, and when I let go of control, this divine energy can guide my life in wonderful ways.*

*Princess dancer of life*

Our bodies are extensions of thought: the soul's thoughts made manifest. Therefore, we have access to miracles, and life itself is proof of this. We can transcend inhibitions and personal obstacles by transcending our minds. We can become free of the physical.

*I can let go of negativity, understanding that negative thinking is the creation of the physical, not the spiritual. I am already free when I transcend my mind and move into the real world that exists beyond fear.*

*Princess detaching from the physical and going within*

Thoughts can dominate a life, but thoughts are not the truth. Having a thought about something does not make it true. Thoughts are happening on the inside, but they do not necessarily come true on the outside. Detaching from the thought and knowing that it does not exist outside of us can result in our seeing a love-based, joyous life. We can live and operate independently of thoughts.

*Having a thought about something does not make it true. I can live free of the limitations of thought. I can transcend thought.*

*Princess aware of a presence*

Sometimes, and often when I am alone, the feeling of presence within me and around me is so powerful it is palpable. I can take time to notice this powerful energy and make it a friend in my life, for I am a part of this mysterious energy.

*Wanting to know my truth, I befriend the mysterious presence that I am aware of when I am alone and quiet.*

# PRINCESS MAZZALOULOU

*Princess releasing the knots felt within*

We can unravel the knots of our minds that create knots in our bodies and hearts, leading to misinterpretation and misperception. We can start to realize the soul's desires by coming into alignment with our life's purpose. Slowly, we begin to feel a lightness in our hearts and bodies as the weight of the physical dissolves. We start to flow through life, guided all the while by a divine force that seems to have everything already planned out.

*I release the knots within me by letting go of life. I can trust that the Universe has a wonderful plan for me and if I relax, I will see it and live it.*

*Princess finding peace and stillness*

The world manifested before our eyes, felt and understood through the senses, is the result of magic and miracles. The world is a sacred place and when we become quiet, we can connect to the rhythm of the Universe: the silent, still, but flowing energy: the place where all that exists comes from.

*When I become quiet and still in my body and mind, I can tune into the truth of the Universe: the powerful sense of peace, silence, stillness and calm that exists everywhere - within me and around me.*

# PRINCESS MAZZALOULOU

*Princess travelling without moving on the magical flying carpet*

We can travel without moving, and we can move without travelling. Of all the places in the world today that Man has explored and journeyed to, surely the most amazing place he discovered was found in his own heart.

*I have seen so much, but I have never travelled far. I have ventured to faraway lands, though all the time I was still. I do not seek, for what I seek, I know does not exist. The most beautiful horizon lies within me and is the resting place where wisdom leads me.*

*Princess feeling the flow of the Universe's energy*

The energy of the Universe is always flowing and creation is born from this energy; we are a part of this creative flow. Energy flows freely through youthful bodies and this can be seen, but as we grow up, energy can stagnate. In order to feel, once again, a part of this exciting energy, we can learn, slowly, to let go of control and hand our lives back to the Universe. Just the tiniest of movements in the direction of this powerful, flowing energy has the ability to create huge shifts in our perception and experience of life.

*If I cling to the reeds by the side of a fast flowing river, I will tire. I will get wet and exhausted, for life cannot flourish under such circumstances of resistance. But, if I let go and go with the flow of the river, and trust, I have opportunities to flourish and experience much, even if I cannot swim.*

# PRINCESS MAZZALOULOU

*Princess knowing and moving with the flow*

Life flows. Seasons flow. Energy flows. Thoughts flow. Time
flows. Waters flow. People can, and do, flow through life:
many do not. When we flow through the tide of life's eternal
flowing energy, we thrive, blossom, and bloom. We radiate a
power and energy reflective of the Universe's divine, mystical
properties for all to see.

*Energy loves to flow through my body, unhindered. When I move my body*
*and relax, energy flows freely and easily. I feel the releasing of negative*
*emotions from tense muscles, and my body and mind feel light and free.*

*Princess dancer of life*

If life were a dance, it would flow. It would beautifully weave and manoeuvre its way in and out of difficult scenarios, effortlessly. We can navigate our way through difficulties in life with ease and dignity when we stay centered within and take our fear out of the equation. Through an internal connectedness akin to a meditation, we can dance through life rather than struggle.

*Whilst it is not easy to remain centered and harmonious within, I can learn not to get caught up in struggles. Life flows through ups and downs like a dance has an ebb and flow, tension and release. I can learn to stay connected to the beautiful dance of life through all situations.*

# PRINCESS MAZZALOULOU

*Princess feeding the animal guests at the window*

The Universe has selected all the right people, circumstances, and places for us to interact with. It is in our alignment with the Universe that we are lead to our own personal best. If we detach from the physical, tune in, and make a deep, personal connection with the Universe, we instinctively know the right path.

*I meet with all the right people, circumstances, and places, when I follow the magical thread of the Universe that weaves itself in, out, around, and through a life designed just for me.*

*Princess making a friend outside the confines of fear*

Once outside our metaphorical window of safety, we step into the unknown, the window of opportunity. We meet with so much magic that we never would have seen had we stayed in our 'house', too afraid to explore 'out there'.

*When I step outside the confines of security and safety, I experience a new reality. I never know what will show up in my life, but whatever happens moment to moment and day by day, it will be wondrous and new.*

# PRINCESS MAZZALOULOU

*Princess releasing her fear of the physical*

The physical gives the illusion of being real, and therefore, having some power over us. But, everything that is physical stems from the spiritual, so in truth, nothing has any power over us. If we test this, we can see that we can live how we want to live without anyone or anything exerting any power over us.

*To live a free, dream-filled life, I release myself from fear. I may feel fear, but I no longer allow it to freeze or immobilize me. I recognize the freeing power fear has, if I befriend it. I watch my fear of the physical dissolve.*

*Princess creating and believing new identities and realities into being*

If we detach ourselves from our identities, who or what we think we are, then we can transform ourselves and our lives. The Universe always supports us and provides a platform upon which we can create the change we would like to see, in our lives and in ourselves.

> *The energy running through me, that is me, has the power to create anything. Therefore, I can let go of identities and beliefs I have about myself and allow the creative force within me to lead me to new realities.*

*Princess focused on joy as she enters the world*

When we step outside our front door, we see signs of fear absolutely everywhere. However, we do not need to pay any attention to them. We can learn to see them for what they are and dismiss them, because as princesses, we want to remain aligned with our happy, joyous vibration.

*I make my home a loving, joyous place to live, filled with good, positive energy. As I leave my house, I tune myself to focus on the beauty that exists in the world. I cast aside the fearful things, for I like to feel happy and free.*

*Princess feeling a naked oneness with the Universe*

If we have created an external identity that we believe internally, then we must always operate in a comfort zone, a place where our identity is in operation and always reinforced. If we were to step outside our comfort zone, we would not know who we are. Therefore, in order to live freely and expansively, and allow the Universe to reveal wonderful insights and show us other possibilities, we need to let go of any artificial identities. Who we are is so much bigger than identity.

*If I am to live all my possibilities, I need to recognize the need to strip away any artificial labels I may have attached to myself. In their place, I can fill up with the acceptance, love, and generosity of the Universe. I can believe in all possibilities and feel a sense of wholeness in all situations.*

*Princess finding the courage to live*

Walking the path of love, freedom, truth, and dreams is difficult, because above all else, it requires courage. Through our bravery, other people can find their courage too. Even vibrationally, our commitment to freedom from fear affects others. Deep down, we are all friends, so we really can ignore the surface tension we experience in life and go in search of a deeper bonding truth.

*I have decided to embrace life with a new perspective. I step out of my outworn ideas and walk courageously in the direction of love, truth, and freedom.*

# THE BEAUTIFUL DANCE OF LIFE

*Princess outside the window of the conventional*

There are different paths in the world, possibilities that we cannot see, or have not seen, for we have only been focusing on what we think is available, or possible, for us. The Universe knows each of us deeply and personally, and has chosen different talents and varied opportunities for each of us. If we have not yet brought our magic to life, then we would not be able to even hazard a guess at what we could contribute to ourselves and the world.

*I dare to think that maybe the Universe has carved out, and created, a path of magic for me. Unless I ask to be shown something dream-filled and wonderful, then I may believe that I'm not one of the lucky ones. No matter what it is, maybe there is a gift for me, that only I would see, my own personal gift from the Universe. I ask to be shown magic.*

# PRINCESS MAZZALOULOU

*Princess serene centered strong and vulnerable*

We are happy because of the way we feel towards someone or something. How someone or something responds to us has nothing to do with us. If we allow other people's vibrations to affect how we feel, we will always be like a leaf blowing around, this way and that way, in the wind. Therefore, in order to feel good within, centered, and in control of our heart, we must acknowledge and own our feelings, even if that makes us feel vulnerable.

*Feeling vulnerable seems like a childlike emotion, and it is. It is a feeling that makes us beautiful on the inside, and the outside, and it is for the strong hearted, born from courage. I admire my ability to stay childlike as an adult and own my vulnerability.*

# THE BEAUTIFUL DANCE OF LIFE

*Princess walking through the open window on a path of love*

We feel safe in our home, it is our sanctuary. The Universe wants us to feel this way wherever we are, safe and happily peaceful. Through trust, we can learn to see the world outside our front door as an extension of our home, a place where we feel loved.

*My home is a place where I can relax and feel happy and safe. I can close my door on the world, but I no longer want to close my door on the world, for I would like to feel happy, relaxed, and safe, everywhere I go. I now create an extension outside my door, a golden path of love that I walk on wherever I go.*

*Princess leaving her comfort zone and living*

When we step outside our comfort zone, our most familiar home, we start to walk a different path that somehow seems guided and destined. We are aware of a presence, and we are aware of impermanence and death. We come to realize that we cannot escape death, and this realization leads us to live life more fully.

*I have confronted my fears by leaving my comfort zone, and I continue every day to confront my fears. I am happy because I recognize the preciousness of life.*

# THE BEAUTIFUL DANCE OF LIFE

*Princess living in the physical and the spiritual*

We can choose to abandon the physical in favor of the spiritual, but we wouldn't really live. And, if we choose to abandon the spiritual, we can become hardened and almost unfeeling. If we recognize that we are spiritual beings in physical bodies, we can learn to move between and integrate the two, finding harmony within ourselves and our lives.

*If I abandon the physical, I don't really live. If I abandon the spiritual, I don't feel much love. If I find balance and harmony between the two, I live as I intended before I came here: I live fully now, but I never forget my true home that is always with me.*

*Princess seeing the outside world as a playground*

If the world were a playground, we could, and would, have fun: we would treat it as such. As adults, we can still see life, and the world, as a place of fun. We manifested ourselves here in order to have fun and enjoy living a physical experience.

*I can take a fresh, new approach to life and see it as a blank canvas upon which to create a fun life. I can add an exciting dimension and fun element to all I do. I can learn to see life as a playground where I enjoy playing freely like a child, and as a result, I will see and feel more love and joy.*

# THE BEAUTIFUL DANCE OF LIFE

*Princess enjoying and exploring the world*

We do not leave our front door and go in search of something, hunting out there for what we feel is missing. If we find what we are looking for inside our four walls, and in the home that lies in our heart, then we are equipped to leave our house and enjoy and explore all the wonderful things of this world.

*I love feeling an ecstatic appreciation for life and all the amazing things of this world. I enjoy the smallest of activities and experiences because I have found peace and comfort in the home of my heart. Now, I can enjoy and explore the good things, people, and places of this world.*

# PRINCESS MAZZALOULOU

*Princess being shown her own personal course in the university of the Universe*

Entering the realm of the Universe is the university that offers everything and so much more. Dreams and life change are offered and new perspectives are guaranteed. It is open to all living things, and it is always free. The only prerequisite is alignment, that we are doing it from our heart and from the truth. If we sincerely want to be shown our own truth and the wonderful path the Universe has planned for us, we only need to let go of control and allow ourselves to be shown and guided.

*I step outside the laws created by fear and see the laws of the Universe in operation. My desire to be educated in the ways of the Universe lead me to a letting go and allowing: the allowing of a loving force much bigger than myself to show me wonderful new ways to live.*

*Princess daring to take her prize from the dreams created by the Universe*

No harm can come to us when we follow the laws of the Universe and step into its world, because everything that happens in this realm, happens in alignment. There are no mistakes or accidents. There is no bad luck or good luck. Everything is destined. Life has secrets waiting to reveal to us when we are ready to see and live.

*There is no luck where some of us win and some of us don't. We all have opportunities and paths that we might follow, if we dare to take the unknown prize. I can take the prize, because I know I will succeed.*

# PRINCESS MAZZALOULOU

*Princess waiting to see the best of everything*

The Universe is a creative force. We can never really know what is going to happen with any degree of certainty until it happens, though it helps to know that alignment is never far away from what we already have. Alignment is the other side of the same coin. The only difference is that feeling alignment with the energy of the Universe, a harmonizing within, feels so good and reveals to us our truth.

*Dreams are a better version of what I already have. It is as though someone fine-tuned my life so I now see the best of everything. When I live at a higher vibration, I consistently feel better than better, I feel great.*

# THE BEAUTIFUL DANCE OF LIFE

*Princess trying out being a cat*

No two lives are the same, so one way of life cannot be applied to all. A spider does not try to be a butterfly, and a bird does not try to be an ant. The world is full of rules about how we should be living, but we do not need to follow them if they do not feel right to us.

*I know that I am being bombarded with information from every source telling me how to live, so I take time to retreat internally and ask myself what is right for me. In a quiet place, I hear the answer.*

# PRINCESS MAZZALOULOU

*Princess dressed like a beautiful cake and feeling full of loving goodness*

Nothing ever really makes us happy. Inner fulfilment, joy, harmony, and peace lead to happiness, and come from the alleviating of pain, the alleviating of pain through a consistent moving towards the truth. Without connectedness, a spiritual connection to the divine, we can sometimes feel like shells, or fancy cakes without a filling.

*It may sound silly, but I am a princess and playful simplicity is my nature, so if I were a cake, I would not only look fancy, I would have a filling, and I would taste great.*

# THE BEAUTIFUL DANCE OF LIFE

*Princess offering thoughts of appreciation to the always listening Universe*

There is a world out there full of things that we can take, but the only things that really fulfil us, are the things that come from love. By making a deep, personal connection within, we can learn to release our desire to keep taking from the world, and instead, allow our gifts to come from the Universe.

*I no longer want to want things I cannot have or that are not meant for me. To be genuinely happy is to allow the Universe to bring me everything when I am in harmony with love. I learn to live by remaining peaceful within and appreciating all that is here with me now.*

# PRINCESS MAZZALOULOU

*Princess climbing through the window of the known to cross the bridge of the unknown*

We no longer have to be prisoners of fear. Countless fairy tales reveal to us that once we are on the other side, we are on the other side. We never have to return to pain once we have dealt with it. There is a bridge that we can cross that leads us from the barren, the dark, and the rocky extremes we find hard to tolerate, and into the beauty of color and light, abundance and joy.

*Instinct, anecdotes, and my own experiences, are proof enough that a magical, free world exists. The magical world is here, and I am brave enough to cross the bridge that leads to it. I do not know how long or treacherous it may be, but knowing that a mysterious, magical word exists the other side, is enough for me to set out on this exciting journey.*

*Princess running home to the elixir of youth*

Fear ages us, there is no doubt about it. Constantly exposing ourselves to stressful situations without allowing ourselves time to recuperate, can leave us feeling and looking drained. Like Cinderella, who turned back into a housemaid at the stroke of midnight, we age and alter if we don't take time out to relax, refresh and revitalize.

*I move through life little step by little step, then I stop to relax. Hurrying through, ultimately slows me down and tires me. My secret to feeling and looking consistently good and youthful is by slowing down, and then slowing down some more. My tiny little efforts produce huge results.*

# PRINCESS MAZZALOULOU

*Princess contorting herself through the window of change*

Change is not easy. We are being born into a new reality. Like the ballet dancer that moves through difficult transitions that look easy, we can move through our internal changes with minimal difficulty. If we shrink our lives and take out all the unnecessary externals, we can transition, with courage, through the changes that are taking place.

*If I recognize that I am changing, and that I am leaving the old behind, I will understand the pain that I am moving through. There is a new reality that lies the other side of pain. Change is a birth into a free me, a dance that I have choreographed. I can identify with the beauty of it rather than the discomfort.*

*Princess traveler on the magic carpet*

If we follow our own personal flow, we will always feel good, for being on our own personal path of flowing energy yields positive results. We are all born travelers because we are spiritual beings living in the midst of a flow of energy. If we live our lives dedicated to staying connected to the flowing energy of the Universe, we are living as true travelers.

*I am a traveler because I follow the flow of the Universe's energy. I need never think about where I am going or who I will meet because it is all there waiting for me as I move through my own personal journey. Every path will unfold with ease and simplicity.*

# PRINCESS MAZZALOULOU

*Princess vulnerable and powerful*

In quiet moments alone, we can tune in and find our truth. To be spiritual is to recognize our innate, mysterious nature and live from that place, seeing the world we live in through the eyes of love, magic, and wonder.

*A blade of grass seems weak as it blows around in the wind, but it is strong. It has an immense connection to all the other blades of grass around it and the soil in which it lives. I, too, may seem weak and vulnerable in a big world, but I have a deep connection to the truth, the love that binds us all, and that makes me immense and powerful. I live my life from that place.*

# THE BEAUTIFUL DANCE OF LIFE

*Princess at one with the free bird and everything*

The bird flying free has no interest in the truth, searching, or looking for a deeper meaning. The bird flying free does not even practice being here now or accepting everything as it is. The bird flying free just "is" and that is why it is free. We can become the free bird.

*In the moment I become present and take it all in, where I witness the magic of the bird flying free, alone, and against the backdrop of a beautiful sunset, I am free of thought. In that instant, I am at one with the bird and everything else. In that moment, I am free.*

# PRINCESS MAZZALOULOU

*Princess zapping problems with her magic wand*

When we leave this world, the things that trouble us now, no longer trouble us, and will never trouble us again. Everything will be gone. Therefore, it is a good idea to make peace in our heart now with all the things we see as problems. We can then really enjoy the experience of living, for that is why we came here.

*I no longer dwell on apparent problems. I decide to believe that there are no problems. I believe that life is a magical illusion where I can wave a wand and all my troubles disappear. When I imagine now that my problems are gone, all of a sudden they are.*

# THE BEAUTIFUL DANCE OF LIFE

*Princess practicing difficult exercises early in the morning in alignment*

We are always in the right place and at the right time, and when we leave this world, we leave at the right time. Therefore, we can enjoy where we are now, because where we are now is exactly where we are meant to be on our journey.

*Where I am now is the place where I am meant to be living. I am aligned with this moment because I am living it. The only way I can get more out of life and live my life to the full, is by fully immersing myself in this magical moment, the moment that is happening right now. I remind myself to enjoy the miracle of this moment that passes so quickly because I do not want to miss a thing.*

# PRINCESS MAZZALOULOU

*Princess enjoying the magic in the miracle of the moment*

Sometimes, we have a strange and mysterious feeling that we have lived this moment before. Outside of what we are currently living exists no-thing, only possible realities. But, these possible realities are our futures and the lives that we planned out before we came here. So, through the experience of de ja vu, we can clearly see that enjoying and loving our creations over feeling negative is preferable. We are experiencing everything the way we do for a reason.

*Whilst having the deeply mysteriously feeling that I have lived this moment before is a little spooky, I recognize the opportunity it gives me to know that struggling is a futile activity. There is no point in pushing against the miracle of the life that I planned for myself. Instead, I can enter into a state of oneness with the Universe and harmonize myself in my current reality, the only place where I find love, joy, and safety.*

# THE BEAUTIFUL DANCE OF LIFE

*Princess preferring to listen to birdsong rather than her own thoughts*

It might be a good idea not to think about, or judge, things as good or bad, light or dark. It might be better not to think at all. If not think, then what? Feel.

*I ask myself, not what I think about something, but rather, how I feel about it. My feelings are a much more reliable guide than my thoughts. Life becomes much easier to navigate when I listen to my feelings over my thoughts, thoughts that I'm not really sure do belong to me.*

# PRINCESS MAZZALOULOU

*Princess sitting at the window ready to move through change*

Though it may seem obvious, we have to be ready for change. Being on the path of change can bring relief even though we may have no idea if, when, or how, change will occur. We are never stuck, we are evolving to the place where we can allow change to enter our lives. We are not outsiders looking in at the miracle of life, we are a part.

*The Universe has not forgotten about me. The Universe is allowing me space to grow. I am not a disregarded member of the human race. If I wish for change to occur and nothing is happening, I am simply being asked to wait. When the time is right I will move through change with ease.*

# THE BEAUTIFUL DANCE OF LIFE

*Princess working with Universal forces to create change*

There is no time limit, or any limit, set by the Universe for the achievement of any goal. If we, one day, decide that we would like to change and walk out into the world a new person, then we can, for the Universe supports all our dreams.

*If I am having a thought that I would like to change something about myself or my life, then I can take small steps now to create the change. I will meet with a positive response from the Universe if I really do want to create change. I need not stay stuck, for I can explore all possibilities.*

# PRINCESS MAZZALOULOU

*Princess looking out of the open window*

We think that we can see and know the world when we look out of our window, but we only really know what is going on when we are living outside the window. Our perspective is often very small and limited due to all the fear based images and messages we are exposed to, but If we step outside our window of perspective, we find that most of what we have been taught, or lead to believe, is false.

*I do not look out of my window, in whatever form, to survey life before I live it. I clear my mind of judgment, I expect the best, and I expect to be wonderfully surprised, for when I do this, life shows me a kind and beautiful world.*

*Princess contemplating exploring the meaning of the synchronicity outside the window*

Coincidence shows us that there is an order to everything. It is as though everything has already been planned in advance of our living it. Nothing is ever just a coincidence, it is more like divine timing or alignment with the Universe. Synchronicity, or coincidence, shows us that there is something mystical and magical going on everywhere and at all times.

*Experiencing coincidence and synchronicity gives me the opportunity to look beyond the surface, physical aspect of life, and open my awareness to a deeper truth that is in operation at all times, knowing this can keep me feeling safe when I become fearful or apprehensive.*

# PRINCESS MAZZALOULOU

*Princess playing the role of princess*

Ultimately, we are not in control, the Universe is. When we relinquish our efforts and surrender to the Universe, we see our deepest, soul level, free from fear, desires manifest. True happiness can never manifest from a manipulated life.

*If life were a theatrical show, I would know instinctively that the actors are not in control, they are playing a role. I know that everything physical is not the truth, and in my physical self, I am essentially playing a role. If I surrender my life to the Universe and live from an authentic place, I experience more magical moments and feel more satisfaction and inner fulfilment.*

# THE BEAUTIFUL DANCE OF LIFE

*Princess and friends eating an elaborate cake that tastes better at its center*

The energy that is the Universe is so amazing and powerful that it creates people, and for that matter, everything, as unique individuals. Therefore, we never need to copy anyone. If we come into alignment with our own miraculous creation, we find magic in our authenticity.

*I find out who I really am, who the Universe and my non-physical self created me to be, when I release anything I may have contrived through my desire to be accepted and good enough. Who I am is much bigger than anything my human efforts can create on their own.*

# PRINCESS MAZZALOULOU

*Princess surrounded only by the truth of now*

If we shrink our lives to the point where all we have in it is what is around us now, we live without confusion, pain, anger and dissatisfaction. We live harmoniously.

*I shrink my life until I no longer look outside of now. I know that I do not really know what will happen next, but I know that it will be the truth. The degree to which I live an authentic life, staying centered in the moment, is the degree to which I find happiness in myself and my life.*

# THE BEAUTIFUL DANCE OF LIFE

*Princess feeding fluffy friends at the window*

Eventually, we find a way out of everything that bothers us. Vibrating on a high frequency, and expecting to love life, princesses believe that something better is always around the corner. We wouldn't make, and then eat, a cake that didn't taste nice. We would discard it.

*I always turn to the best of everything. If something becomes bothersome, I turn again, for I live my life by following the best of everything.*

# PRINCESS MAZZALOULOU

*Princess cat and spider the lucky ones*

We are the lucky ones if we notice the sun shining, the tree growing, or the spider on its web. If, when we step outside our door, we smell the air, we are the lucky ones. Nature is the Universe's most magnificent creation, we can learn much from Nature.

*Even if I don't notice anything else, I notice Nature in all its forms. Nature teaches me that I am never alone. The tree stands alone, but it is not alone. The spider lives alone on its web, but it is not alone. I stand alone, but I am not alone. I am a part of Nature's oneness.*

# THE BEAUTIFUL DANCE OF LIFE

*Princess paper dolls remnants from the past being left behind*

To move through the open window of change and emerge the other side a fresh, new person, we need to go of accumulated worries from the past. We are not the past, or someone else's opinion of us. We are not our thoughts or our past behavior. We are all made of love, and we all have the capacity to act from that place. Love is what enables us to change.

*Instead of assuming I am a whole string of negative labels, I assume I am a creation made by something deeply mysterious and intangible. I assume I am loved and worthy, forgiven and accepted, because the love the Universe has for me is always pure, accepting, and free flowing.*

# PRINCESS MAZZALOULOU

*Princess in spirit form*

We could be anybody. Underneath the disguise of the roles we play, or the work we identify ourselves with, or the company we keep, or the possessions we have, or the clothes we wear, we could be anybody, and we are. We are all deeply mysterious and otherworldly, masquerading as people.

*I could be anybody inside my four walls. It is only on entering the physical world that I become physical, a "this" or a "that", a label. But I am much, much more, and I now connect to the deeper, real me, the place where I feel whole.*

# THE BEAUTIFUL DANCE OF LIFE

*Princess fleeing into a magical world*

It seems silly to criticize ourselves. After all, who are we criticizing? And who is doing the criticizing? In fact, can any person, thing, behavior, situation be judged and criticized. What happens when we can no longer judge or criticize? Acceptance.

*In truth, not even acceptance happens when I find everything beyond judgment and criticism. There is nothing, just an inner knowing that everything is exactly as it is meant to be. Interestingly, I do not enter into a place of confusion, I enter into a magical place that, again, cannot be deciphered, for to do so would be to judge. In the absence of judgment, I enter, through a magic window, into a mystical world.*

# PRINCESS MAZZALOULOU

*Princess meeting a harvest mouse*

With a connection to the Universe, we feel whole. Loneliness is only something we feel in the absence of a connection, and it is usually attached to something external. If we incorporate our home into our heart and live from that place, we need never feel alone again.

*I like to feel warm and cozy like a harvest mouse in its snugly nest. I make a home inside myself where I always feel cozy and warm. I can then travel anywhere and do anything with a smile on my face because I have a secret home.*

# THE BEAUTIFUL DANCE OF LIFE

*Princess and cat dancing*

We do not need to spend years evolving, or commit hours of time working through buried pain in order to feel love and happiness, though sometimes this is necessary. Everybody feels sheer bliss at times, and if, when that happens, we recognize it, and genuinely wish to live in that place, we just need to ask. We will find that the Universe starts to reveal to us more scenarios in which we can connect to joy.

*I do not always need to assume I am far, far away from feeling love and joy. If I recognize and remember joy, love, and bliss, and hold onto that feeling, expecting more, I trust that I will eventually make that place my permanent home.*

# PRINCESS MAZZALOULOU

*Princess stepping out of the old and into the new*

We need to step out of the person we think we are and into the person we imagine we would like to be, the person we know we can be. That person lives inside of us and wants to be released, only our fearful self prevents it from happening.

*The Universe supports all my dreams. I have dreams for a reason. Any dream can be realized with my commitment, staying in alignment with the signs of the Universe, letting go of control, and having the courage to step into a new unrealized self.*

*Princess leaf that freed herself*

We don't have to live like a leaf on the ground, always being trodden on. We can attract a gust of wind that blows us out of the path of destruction and onto open, green spaces where we can live free and breathe easily.

*I don't need to get caught up in the hustle and bustle of life. I can travel on the quieter path and still participate. I do not have to follow the crowd if I don't want to. The Universe accepts me and gives me permission to be me. I can be the lucky, happy, free leaf.*

# PRINCESS MAZZALOULOU

*Princess being held by the Universe*

In order for the Universe to work its magic in our lives, we need to let go of that which no longer serves a purpose, or enriches us at a deep level, that which has no substance. If we are brave and sit with not-knowing, something must change.

*I'm going to see today as the first day of my life where I now know nothing about what the future holds for me, and live with that acceptance. The only thing that can really keep something in my life is love, for nothing can keep nothing in my life when I let go of control.*

*Princess evolving her fears*

If we want to hand control of our lives over to the Universe and follow our dreams, we have to overcome our fears, and that includes fear of death. We have dreams, but the Universe has ultimate control. Only the Universe knows where we are going. So, we dream, and in the process of realizing our dreams, we relinquish control and release our fears.

*If I allow fear the time and space, it eventually dominates my life and halts my progress. So, I keep moving forward, despite my fear, and I am usually pleasantly surprised by its disintegration into nothing.*

# PRINCESS MAZZALOULOU

*Princess flowing with the river of life*

With a strong connection to Nature and purpose, we flow. We naturally feel that a flowing river flows supports life in a way that stagnant waters do not, and so it is the same with us. When we listen to our own individual cues given by the Universe regarding what to do, where to go, and how to live, we can expect to flow. Our life becomes divinely guided.

*When I flow with life, I know it. I feel healthier, more vibrant and alive. The energy running through me feels as though it is flowing and nourishing every cell in my body. I feel good, and feeling good is my purpose.*

# THE BEAUTIFUL DANCE OF LIFE

*Princess looking out her window expecting a good day*

Before we step outside our door, we expect to have a good day, but it doesn't always turn out that way. It can be difficult when outside our home to stay centered in our own energy, but we can. If we see our life as precious, and believe we are here to be happy, we should make feeling good our highest priority.

*Before I step outside my door, I consciously remind myself to stay feeling good, no matter what happens. I believe I have a right to be happy, so I maintain my connection to joy by remaining connected to my own energy and purpose.*

*Princess as eternal child*

Children are happy and free-spirited. They love life, and that is why they look young and energetic. Why would we ever want to grow up?

*I have observed that a princess is an eternal child. It is my intention therefore, to be a little girl forever, to be a princess. Life is meant to be forever wondrous.*

*Princess seeing friends on the horizon*

Sometimes, we wish to see, but we cannot. We wish to understand, but we do not understand. How then do we see? How then do we understand? We look. We look until we see.

*There are things I feel confused about. I feel lost and I don't understand. I trust that if I continue to look, I will one day see. I will one day understand. The Universe has the ability to tune my senses so that what was once impossible to comprehend, is now as clear as day.*

# PRINCESS MAZZALOULOU

*Princess alone outside at night*

We don't need to walk through life feeling suspicious. We are always protected by the Universe. Snow White was never on her guard despite obvious threats. She was open and trusting. Therefore, no harm could befall her. We can trust too that we wear an invisible veil of protection and it is called the love of the Universe.

*I do not need proof that I am loved, guided, and protected, for I just know instinctively that I am. With my trust and faith in the Universe, I can walk a safe path through life.*

# THE BEAUTIFUL DANCE OF LIFE

*Princess seeking out a wise person*

Nothing lasts forever. Everybody loses so much along their journey through life, and when we recognize that everything that happened in the past is over, we can enjoy, so much more, the good things that are with us now. Life was never meant to be permanent.

*There is a time limit for everyone. I cannot seek out a wise and gifted being that dwells in the hills who can extend my life via some magical elixir. My life will be completed when I leave. So, I remember that nothing ever lasts, and I learn to savor the events of my life whilst they are happening.*

# PRINCESS MAZZALOULOU

*Princess joining the journey*

Frightening though it may be, we are all here together to travel the journey of life. It is far more exciting, and reduces our fear, to be the traveler we were born to be rather than a fearful onlooker. The Universe has made some exciting plans for each of us and promises its love for the whole of the journey.

*I no longer feel scared to free myself from a life that keeps me stuck. No matter how small, or big, my journey will be, I feel I will be safe. I have nothing to lose by taking one step at a time in a forward direction, through life, with faith.*

*Princess freeing a caged bird*

If we don't think outside of what is happening now, we don't feel pain. It requires discipline, but we can learn to do it until it is second nature. Everything that is not happening now is not relevant to this moment. And for our happiness, it is essential we free ourselves from the mind's ever worrying thoughts.

*If I release my bird from its cage, I think I have given it freedom as I watch it fly away. But, what good to the bird is its freedom if its mind is still in the cage?*

# PRINCESS MAZZALOULOU

*Princess really interacting with her environment*

One day we come to realize that nothing out there can fix our loneliness, low mood, or anxiety, and that realization can make us feel worse. It is hard to fix something on the inside, or is it? When we really connect with what is happening now, we start to fill up with the warm feeling that was missing. It is as though we have lit a fire in a cold room.

*I connect to love by connecting to my present experiences. When I stroke my cat, I really stroke my cat. When I drink tea, I really drink tea. I make every action magical, and before long, my heart, mind, and body feel warmed.*

*Princess and rain*

If it were to rain today, we would put up our umbrellas. But, if we were to experience much negativity today, we would, most likely, absorb it. How foolish we are to remain physically dry but allow our spirits to be dampened.

*When life rains down showers of negativity, I put my internal umbrella up because I like to stay nice and dry on the inside.*

# PRINCESS MAZZALOULOU

*Princess and the rainbow called hope*

There is nothing wrong with hope, if hope makes us feel happy. One day, who knows when, hope will manifest. Hope is like the rainbow that holds a pot of gold at its end just waiting for us to find it. The sun must always come out again once the rain has passed.

*Sometimes, I feel that holding onto hope is hopeless. But what is wrong with hope if it makes me feel happy? I came here to wish and dream, for wishing and dreaming, for their own sake, enables me to live in a magical world.*

# THE BEAUTIFUL DANCE OF LIFE

*Princess holding onto her vision of another life*

If we hold a vision of another life, or the person we would like to be, or something we wish for, then the Universe will show us the steps to take in order to get there. It can be difficult to hold the vision, but we must train ourselves to believe more in our inner vision than our outer vision and reality.

*I move towards my inner vision by holding onto it in my mind's eye and taking the path the Universe lays out for me. I learn to pay more attention to my inner reality and dreams.*

# PRINCESS MAZZALOULOU

*Princess living in the home within*

When we feel inner unrest, we can easily stay stuck in that place, but anxiety is just a mindset, and any state of mind can be changed in an instant. However, it is not usually that easy if we do not have access to strategies that work. One way to alleviate anxiety, is to become quiet within and connect to a deep, peaceful truth. Through trusting the peace within, we can move through difficulties much easier.

*If I practice going within to a place where I feel safe, I begin to find a home that I can trust in where the noise around me disappears. In time, I can live my whole life connected to the peace that lives deep within me.*

*Princess connected to her own love*

If we are being true to ourselves and living an honest life, we have absolutely nothing to worry about. We can step outside our door and brush aside any negativity easily, because living an honest life is to walk with peace in our heart.

*I think I am being true to myself and living an honest life, I can do nothing more. If I accept myself, then I do not really need anyone else's approval. I can walk on this earth and feel at peace with myself because I have my own love and acceptance.*

# PRINCESS MAZZALOULOU

*Princess knowing the truth lies within*

When we know who we are, life becomes much more exciting. We are made of miracles and magic. When we know that everything physical is such a miraculous design that we wholly believe in it, we cannot help but marvel at the creation of life.

*I know that life is like a dream, a grand illusion created by a divine, mystical force. I believe I am real and therefore, I must be, but not so much at a physical level, rather, at a deep level. My physical self is nothing more than the icing on a beautiful cake.*

# THE BEAUTIFUL DANCE OF LIFE

*Princess dropping the sack from the past*

We are walking around with past disappointments, guilt, anger, and regrets, and whilst there is nothing wrong with feeling our emotions, to carry them around with us throughout the rest of our lives is just plain foolish. We wouldn't carry all our heavy, unwanted belongings from the past around with us in a big sack every day. In order to be free and live an unburdened life where we really can connect to the beauty of this world, we need to drop off our heavy sack, our weighty loads, for they have no purpose anymore, and probably never did.

*It is so easy to leave behind my sack full of unwanted emotional burdens from the past, I just need to put it down, though it seems something prevents me. All I need is time and space to let go as well as the willingness to believe in my right to be happy and free. The Universe supports me and will always be there to assist me in my letting go.*

# PRINCESS MAZZALOULOU

*Princess shining out the light within*

There are certain characteristics that we would rather not attribute to ourselves, and we can free ourselves of these unwanted qualities by being aware of them. If we recognize that we have started to feel insecure, we can turn our inner light on. When our inner light is on, we are always the most beautiful person. Even if everyone else has their inner light on, we will all be the most beautiful shining light in the room, such is the power of light, love, and magic.

*If I feel insecure, I recognize it. I tune myself to the light of love within, and shine it out for all to see.*

*Princess seeing through the eyes of the Universe*

Whenever I see something as bad, or going wrong, I am judging. How do I know whether something is going wrong? When it seems as though things are going wrong, it does not necessarily mean they are. Sometimes, it is part of our path for things to take a path we had not foreseen, or expected. In the eyes of the Universe, nothing ever goes wrong.

*If, in the eyes of the Universe, nothing ever goes wrong, then that is confirmation enough that all is going along just fine. I now choose to see that nothing ever goes wrong.*

# PRINCESS MAZZALOULOU

*Princess sending her pain out to sea*

We can always relive the past, anytime we want. We can always conjure up regrets and painful hurts, but why? There comes a time in our lives when we need to put everything that hurts into a little box and send it out to sea where it can drift away beyond the horizon, out of our hearts and minds, no longer to be seen or felt, for the past has no bearing on the present.

*I only stay stuck in the past because I keep reliving it in my mind. I am free to live when I recognize that the past is no longer here. I can let the painful memories go.*

*Princess always accepted always divinely timed*

We can feel confident and good about ourselves all the time when we recognize that we are never rejected. If we are denied opportunities, it is because we either do not really want what we are asking for, or our timing is off. If, in our feeling of rejection, we internalize it, we become stuck. To flow effortlessly through life is to recognize that we are never rejected or cast out, and if we feel we have been, we just need to extend many more loving thoughts and gestures towards ourselves.

*Seeing clearly the truth of a situation is difficult if I am feeling unwanted or rejected. Therefore, I always look for opportunities to see the situation differently. I explore the possibility that I am either not ready for the change I seek, or that maybe I am taking the wrong route. I know that the Universe always exceeds my limited expectations, so I trust in the design.*

*Princess being invited into a magical world by a mysterious being*

Everything happens at the open window, the portal into another world. Our experience of life depends upon whether we stay the safe side of the window or have the courage to go through. Ultimately we never have anything to lose by exploring another path, another possibility.

*I imagine a world ruled by magic, love, and miracles. I imagine mystical, benevolent beings of all different kinds inviting me to join their world, the world that only knows a reign of harmony and joy. Then I remember that I already live in that world, I just need to keep fine tuning my perspective and travel through the open window, the portal that will show me something new.*

# THE BEAUTIFUL DANCE OF LIFE

*Princess learning from the animals*

We came to live in this world with a purpose. Like animals live to work, survive, and reproduce, we are much the same. Our purpose in life is often woven through our work. Through work, we can express our deepest selves and our deepest ideas.

*Animals are simple creatures with simplistic lives, and life itself is simple for me when I live with simple values. To follow my dreams is to live a simple life. Like the mighty, proud eagle who lives a life of ease and simplicity, I can hold my head up and feel at peace with myself when I follow my own path, and live my own purpose.*

# PRINCESS MAZZALOULOU

*Princess entering a world of many exciting choices*

We should always take responsibility for our actions. If we do something and afterwards feel guilty, we are not being kind to ourselves. We need to immerse ourselves fully in the moment of whatever it is we are doing and know we are making a choice. We can be free to choose and we can be free of guilt.

*Everything I do, I do because I want to. I free myself from the potential struggle in all situations and make my decisions from a place of choice. There is a world full of things outside my window, so I get clear in my mind what I want and what I do not want, and therein I free myself of the burden of guilt.*

# THE BEAUTIFUL DANCE OF LIFE

*Princess learning to understand the world in which she lives*

We need understanding. When we understand, we no longer blame. Understanding comes through our becoming quiet within and our willingness to learn. When we do understand, we let go. We experience an internal shift where we see the generous nature of the Universe.

*When I understand the reason for something happening in my life, I am set free. I am released. The Universe is an extremely benevolent, creative, loving force that supports me. Therefore, there is never anyone or anything to blame. I am free when I become quiet and understand.*

# PRINCESS MAZZALOULOU

*Princess pushing at the window of change*

If we are wishing for change, we need to take small steps in the direction of change. One day, we will see something new on the horizon, for if we keep pushing at an invisible barrier that stands between ourselves and the change we would like to see, we will eventually get to the other side.

*I have not, as yet, been witness to the me that exists in my mind, but I believe my faith and willingness to keep applying pressure to the invisible window will eventually reveal a whole new reality. Something else will appear on my horizon.*

*Princess making a huge cake based on a tiny cake*

If we are not creating a life we love, or worse, we have given up, it could be because we do not believe we have enough power to change. But, the very fact that we are alive proves we have access to vast amounts of power, and if we direct our power purposefully, we can create so much.

*Every tiny action I take is proof that I can make decisions and carry them out. I can now extend this idea by making changes in my life that I once thought were impossible. If I can make tiny changes, I can, with a little more work, make big changes.*

# PRINCESS MAZZALOULOU

*Princess and her beauty treatment*

True beauty is something that comes from the inside and shines out, and we all have access to that inner light. When we are constantly turning towards joy and inner harmony, we feel happy, and it is the happiness that comes from being focused on what we enjoy that makes us attractive and keeps us looking young.

*I do not need to seek out anything physical to keep me beautiful and young. If I felt joyous, happy, whole and in harmony with myself, I could walk around in a sack and I would look beautiful and glow. My best beauty treatment is to feel inner love, contentment, and peace.*

*Princess freeing herself through a princess approach to life*

If, when we feel lost, alone, and afraid in the world, we do something for ourselves that makes us feel special, like a princess, we automatically move onto a higher vibration. We deserve our own love, and we deserve to let in the love of the Universe.

*I can heal, and I can feel whole and loved when I believe I am worthy of my own love and the love of the Universe. When I treat myself like a princess, I instantly feel better.*

*Princess healing through sleep*

No matter how difficult something that we are going through may be, there is always healing available. Sleep and relaxation are amazing at healing our bodies and minds. Tension and fearful thoughts can create problems, but through the letting go that relaxation and sleep require, we recharge, renew and recuperate. We are restored to good health.

*I make sleep and relaxation a very important part of my day, for I cannot function effectively if I feel tired, stressed, and worn. All healing takes place through sleep and relaxation, and as a consequence, my energy levels increase.*

*Princess finding peace in Nature*

At the end of all the searching, there is Nature. Nature is our gift from the Universe. If we have a connection to Nature, we can do anything, travel anywhere, and obtain anything, and there is always a home for us. When all has been done, we come home to Nature.

*In my attempt to find life, happiness, and a meaning, I went searching. At the end of all my searching, I found Nature. It was where I began and it is where it I end. If I come to that end, I have found true peace, and true peace is what I truly desire.*

# PRINCESS MAZZALOULOU

*Princess flying free through the window*

We need to be ready for change. All the internal changes need to have happened in order for us to see the change we desire manifest in reality. When that day comes, we step into a new life, the shift has happened. All the preparation has finally culminated in our being rewarded. We now know that trust in the process is key to seeing real, positive change in our lives.

*I can walk, with peace in my heart, through the open window that awaits me now that I have created shifts inside myself. I have worked hard on the inside and healed myself from my past. I can now live the life that was once only a tiny dream but grew through my consistent trust. I am free.*

# PRINCESS MAZZALOULOU

# THE BEAUTIFUL DANCE OF LIFE

*Princess Mazzaloulou*

# PRINCESS MAZZALOULOU

# THE BEAUTIFUL DANCE OF LIFE

.

Made in the USA
Charleston, SC
30 December 2016